ISBN 0-89820-129-2

Record Research Inc.
P.O. Box 200
Menomonee Falls, Wisconsin 53052-0200   U.S.A.

Phone: 414-251-5408
Fax: 414-251-9452
E-Mail: record@execpc.com
Web site: http://www.recordresearch.com

Joel Whitburn's

4th Edition

Top Country Singles

1944-1997

Billboard

Chart Data Compiled From *Billboard's* Country Singles Charts, 1944-1997